ROBERT BURNS

This edition first published in 1996 by
Lindsay Publications
Glasgow G14 9NP

ISBN 1 898169 07 1

A CIP record of this book is available
from the British Library

Typeset in 15/20pt Caxton
Designed by Janet Watson
Graphic reproduction by Mitchell Graphics, Glasgow

Printed and bound by Oriental Press, U.A.E.

ROBERT BURNS

The Story of
Scotland's National Poet

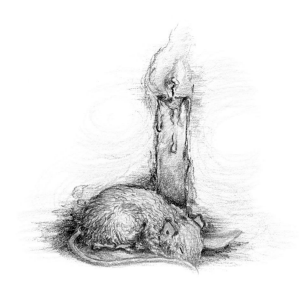

Judith Paterson
Illustrated by Michaela Paterson

LINDSAY
PUBLICATIONS

Robert Burns was born in Alloway, on a cold, wet and windy night. It was January the 25th, 1759.

Today, over two hundred years later, he is remembered as Scotland's Bard, the national poet.

His family called him Robin. He grew up on a farm with his brothers and sisters, and the children helped their mother look after the cows and chickens. She sang as she worked, making butter and cheese. Robert loved to hear her old folk songs.

When he was grown up he wrote a poem about the night he was born. That night an old lady came to visit and looked at his palm. She saw he would be no fool and everyone would be proud of him.

The poem was written using old Scottish words:

"The gossip keekit in his loof,
        (peeped,   palm)
Quo' scho, Wha lives will see the proof,
(spoke, she,   who)
This waly boy will be nae coof,
        (sturdy,   no,   fool)
I think we'll ca' him Robin."
        (call)

from: *Rantin, Rovin, Robin. . .*

Sometimes an old cousin, Betty Davidson, came to stay with the family. Robert always wanted to hear her wild stories about witches and devils, kelpies and ghosts, fairies and brownies. These were the folk tales of the countryside and they were scary.

Robert's father did not approve of such stories. He sent the boys to school to learn about the important things in the world.

Many years later though, Robert still remembered Betty's ghosts and devils, and he filled his poems with all these mysterious, ghostly creatures.

Stories about the ruined Kirk in Alloway were always favourites. Once the village people thought the devil had been trapped inside! They thought they could see his horns through the windows and they heard terrible noises. Throughout the night they stayed inside their houses in fear of the monster. In the morning, all they found was a poor frightened cow.

Robert was seven when his family moved to a new farm, Mount Oliphant. He and his brother Gilbert helped every day before they went to school. They learned to plough and to bring in the harvest. It was very hard work for a small boy,

In the fields, Robert watched the birds, saw the little field mice and listened to the new born lambs. He loved the world around him and was sorry when he ploughed up a Mountain Daisy:

"Wee, modest, crimson-tipped flow'r,
(tiny)
Thou's met me in an evil hour;
(you)
For I maun crush amang the stoure
    (must,   among,   stones)
Thy slender stem. . ."
(your)
from: *To a Mountain Daisy*

     Years later Robert wrote many poems about such simple things. People understood what he was saying. They, too, had accidentally crushed pretty flowers when they were working.

When Robert was seventeen his father sent him to the little town of Kirkoswald to study mathematics. He lived with his aunt. Robert worked hard but he also had fun. It was his first chance to see a wider world.

People treated him as a young man and he felt very grown-up. When he went to the tavern, he spoke with smugglers who brought brandy from the pirate ships and he met Souter Johnnie and the McTaggarts of Shanter Farm.

Later on, Robert remembered all this when he wrote his poems:

"Fast by an ingle, bleezing finely,
(close to the hearth)
Wi' reaming swats, that drank divinely;
(with foaming beer)
And at his elbow, Souter Johnny,
(shoemaker)
His ancient, trusty, drouthy crony."
(thirsty   friend)

from: *Tam O'Shanter*

It was exciting for a young lad to be sitting and talking with such interesting people.

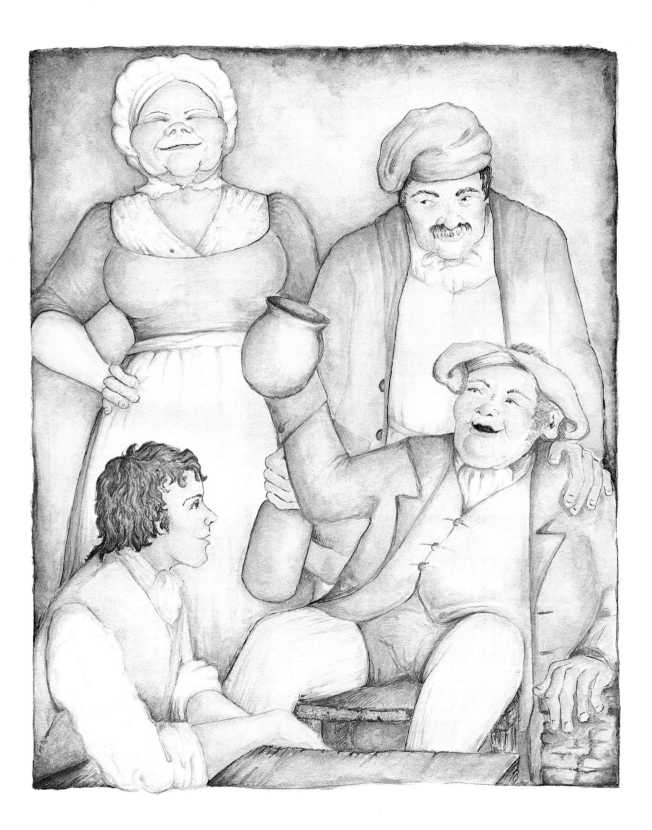

The family moved to Lochlie Farm, near the town of Tarbolton, when Robert was 18. Though most young men had their hair cut short, he grew his hair long and tied it back with a ribbon. He wore a fancy cloak of rusty red while most lads wore grey. Robert was a rebel.

He began to write poems: some made his friends laugh; others made them think. They might be poor folk, but Robert knew they were real men. He wanted them to be proud of their simple honest lives.

"What though on hameley fare we dine,
          (homely,   food)
Wear hoddin grey, an a' that?
     (home-made cloth)
Gie fools their silks, and knaves their wine,
(give)
A man's a man for a' that."

from: *A Man's a Man*

"In Tarbolton, ye ken, there are proper young men,
          (know)
And proper young lasses and a' man,"

"There' ane they ca' Jean, I'll warrant ye've seen,
     (one,   call)
As bonie a lass or as braw, man."
     (bonnie,   fine)

from: *The Ronalds of the Bennals*

After his father died, Robert became head of the household. He was twenty-five when, with his brother, bought Mossgiel, a new farm for the family.

Robert fell in love with his "Bonie Jean":

"There was a lass, and she was fair:
At kirk and market to be seen,
When a' our fairest maids were met,
The fairest maid was bonie Jean."

from: *Bonie Jean*

At Mossgiel, Robert wrote epistles or letters in verse. He made fun of the pompous minister and that made people laugh. He wrote many poems for the pretty girls of the village but it was Jean he loved and married:

"O my Luve's like a red, red rose
That's newly sprung in June;
O my Luve's like the melodie
That's sweetly play'd in tune."

from: *A Red, Red Rose*

Robert first met Jean at a dance. The next time he saw her she was washing clothes by the stream and his puppy trampled over her clean washing. Jean was very cross!

Soon Robert had so many poems his friends advised him to get them printed. Robert's book, *"Poems, Chiefly in the Scottish Dialect"* was published on July 31st, 1786.

One of his best-loved poems is called *"To a Mouse"*, written after he had ploughed up its nest. No-one would really want to hurt such a tiny creature:

> "Wee, sleekit, cowrin, tim'rous beastie,
> O, what a panic's in thy breastie!"

> "Thy wee bit housie, too, in ruin!"

How people laughed at his poem, *"To a Louse"*. They could imagine the wee louse on the fancy hat of the grand lady:

> "Ha! whare ye gaun, ye crowlin ferlie?
>   *(going,   crawling, wonder)*
> Your impudence protects you sairly,"
>   *(cheekiness,   surely)*
> "I wad na been surpris'd to spy
> You on an auld wife's flainen toy;
>   *(old,   flannel cap)*
> But Miss's fine Lunardi! fye!
>   *(fashionable bonnet)*
> How daur ye do't?"
>   *(dare)*

When all the books were sold, people wanted more, so Robert borrowed a pony and rode into Edinbugh to find a publisher. For a young farmer this was a real adventure. He arrived on a grey November evening in 1786.

The city was crowded with tall buildings and narrow streets. It was very different from the green countryside but Robert loved it.

He met many interesting and famous people. William Creech agreed to publish the Edinburgh edition of his book. Robert wrote a poem about Edinburgh, or "Edina" as he called the city. He was so pleased that people in this famous city welcomed a country boy:

"Edina! Scotia's darling seat!
(Scotland's favourite centre)
All hail thy palaces and tow'rs,"

"Thy sons, Edina, social, kind,
With open arms the stranger hail;"
from: *Address to Edinburgh*

Robert became famous. He was an unusual man: a ploughboy who was a poet.

"My father was a farmer upon the Carrick border, O,
And carefully he bred me in decency and order, O."

from: *My Father was a Farmer*

Robert, still the rebel, played the part and dressed in buckskin trousers and boots instead of stockings and shoes. The newspapers wrote stories about him. Many people, including the rich and powerful, bought his book because they wanted to read about Scotland, the land, and its people.
Robert had been granted his dearest wish:

"That I for poor auld Scotland's sake
Some usefu' plan or book could make,
Or sing a sang at least."

from: *To Mrs Scott*

Of course Robert couldn't resist making fun of these wealthy, well educated folk:

"What's a' your jargon o' your schools,
Your Latin names for horns an' stools?
If honest Nature made you fools,
What sairs your grammars?"
         (serves,   text books)

from: *Epistle to J.Lapraik*

Now that he had some money, Robert decided to travel. He wandered all over Scotland; from the beautiful Borders to the rugged Highlands:

> "Amang thae wild mountains shall still be my path,
> *(those)*
> Ilk stream foaming down its ain green, narrow strath."
> *(Every,   own,   valley)*
>
> from: *Yon Wild Mossy Mountains*

He visited the famous sites of Bannockburn and Culloden where, years before, brave Scots had fought battles. Because he was proud of these heroes, Robert wrote the poem *"Bruce To His Men At Bannockburn."*

> "Scots, wha hae wi' Wallace bled,
> *(who, have, with)*
> Scots, wham Bruce has often led. . ."
> *(whom)*

Robert wrote about the mountains, the valleys and the lochs of the Highlands where he was invited to stay with clan chiefs in their castles:

"Wherever I wander, wherever I rove,
The hills of the Highlands for ever I love."

from: *My Heart's in the Highlands*

While he travelled, Robert had plenty of time to think about his songs and poems. He remembered the stories of his childhood, especially the devil in Kirk Alloway. He thought about all the interesting people he'd met in Kirkoswald. He composed one of his best-known poems and filled it with all the scary things he had loved as a small boy.

Tam O' Shanter
After the market, Tam had stayed at the tavern, drinking until it was late. By the time he had to ride home there was a storm.

Tam was scared, watching:

"lest bogles catch him unawares:
  (hobgoblins)
Kirk-Alloway was drawing nigh,
Whare ghaists and houlets nightly cry"
  (ghosts,   owls)

And sure enough:

"And, vow! Tam saw an uno sight!
          (unwelcome)
Warlocks and witches in a dance;"

One of the witches was dancing in her short shift or
cutty-sark, and she was so good Tam forgot where he was
and he yelled:

". . . 'Weel done, Cutty-sark!'
And in an instant all was dark;"

The terrible chase began. Tam was saved
by galloping fast across the river
but his horse had to leave
behind her tail!

Robert decided to become an Exciseman, an "inspector" for the Government. He rode around the country looking for smugglers, checking taverns and even people's houses to see if they were making whisky. They had to have a licence to do this. He knew the people did not like the Excise and in one of his songs he imagined how pleased the smugglers would be if the devil ran off with the Exciseman:

"The deil's awa, the deil's awa,
    (devil's, away)
The deil's awa wi' th' Exciseman!
We'll mak our maut, and we'll brew our drink,
    (make,   malt,)
We'll laugh, sing, and rejoice, man,
And monie braw thanks to the meikle black Deil,
    (many, hearty,   big)
That danc'd awa wi' th' Exciseman."

from: The Deil's Awa wi' th' Exciseman

Sometimes Robert was out riding from dawn until very late at night. Although it was pleasant when the sun shone, it could also be hard and lonely work. Often he had to ride through the dark and stormy winter weather.

All the hard work made Robert ill but he needed a good job to support his family of five children. He was pleased when the Excise transferred him to Dumfries, in 1791.

After a day's work Robert's great joy was to write his songs and poems but he thought it was wrong to write for money:

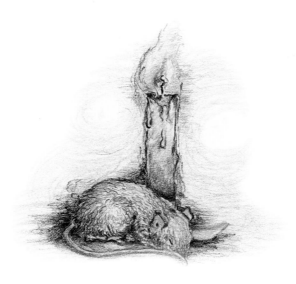

"Some rhyme (vain thought!) for needfu' cash;
(needful)
Some rhyme to court the countra clash, . .
(attract country gossip)
For me, an aim I never fash;
(think of)
I rhyme for fun."

from: *Epistle to James Smith*

Robert could still make people laugh, even at his toothache:

"My curse upon your venom'd stang,
(poisoned, sting)
That shoots my tortur'd gooms alang.."
(gums) *(along)*

from: *Address to the Toothache*

The year was 1793 and Britain was at war with France so Robert ended this poem by wishing all Scotland's enemies a twelvemonth toothache!

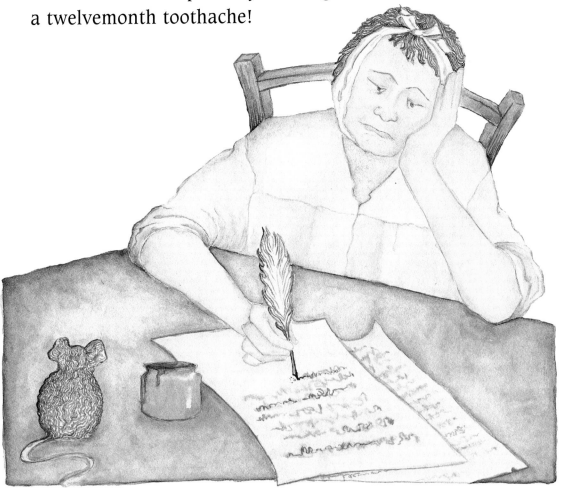

Robert had learned to play the fiddle and he collected over a hundred songs that were published in *"The Scots Musical Museum"*. He wanted these old songs saved for the children of the future:

"I am a fiddler to my trade,
An a' the tunes that e'er I play'd
The sweetest still to wife or maid,
Was 'Whistle owre the lave o't'."
                    (over the rest of it)

from: *The Jolly Beggars*

Robert died on July 21st,1796.

Rantin, Rovin, Robin had a hard life but the old gossip's words had come true:

"He'll hae misfortunes great an' sma'
        (have,   small)
But ay a heart aboon them a'.
        (always,   above,   all)
He'll be a credit till us a':
                (to us all)
We'll a' be proud o' Robin!''

from: *Rantin, Rovin, Robin*

All these years later, Robert Burns is known as Scotland's Bard. To celebrate his birthday people have **Burns Suppers**. They eat haggis, one of Robert's favourite Scottish dishes. How many poets write a poem to a pudding ?

"Fair fa' your honest, sonsie face,
Great Chieftain o' the Puddin'-race!"

from: *Address to a Haggis*

It is a chance to listen to his wonderful poetry. It is a time to laugh and to sing but it is also a time to think as well. Robert truly believed men are brothers and should be friends. It was one of his greatest beliefs:

"For a' that an' a' that,
It's comin yet for a' that,
That man to man, the world o'er,
Shall brithers be for a' that."
     (brothers)

from: *A Man's a Man*

Each New Year, people round the world join hands and sing Robert's song, *Auld Lang Syne*: they remember old friends near and far; they hope for happiness, laughter and peace. Robert's wish, to "make a useful song", came true, not just for Scotland, but for the world.